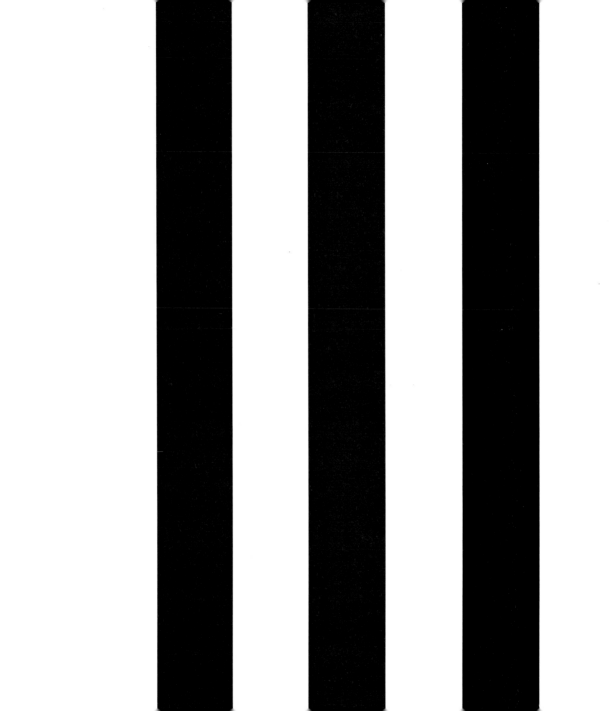

C is for Cat *An Alphabet Album*

For Madame Redkatski

C is for Cat *An Alphabet Album*

By Pamela Prince Photographs by Doug Benezra

Harmony Books New York

Published by Harmony Books
201 East 50th Street,
New York, New York 10022.
Member of the
Crown Publishing Group.

Harmony and colophon are
trademarks of Crown Publishers, Inc.

Manufactured in Hong Kong

Prince, Pamela.
C is for Cat / An Alphabet Album
by Pamela Prince;
photographs by Doug Benezra.--1st ed.
p.   cm.

1.Cats--Poetry. 2.Cats--Pictorial works.
3.Alphabet rhymes.
I. Benezra, Doug. II. Title.
PS3566.R573A62 1992
811'.54--dc20   91-42179   CIP AC

ISBN 0-517-58563-4

Designed by Michael Mabry

10 9 8 7 6 5 4 3 2 1

First Edition

A  Z

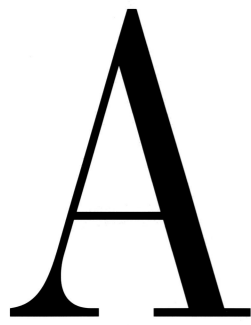 is for Annabelle,

ball of fur,
small and soft,
one look at her
might make anybody
want to purr
and charm every
pussycat connoisseur.

B is for Boris,
　　　　substantial and gray,
with a stare he employs
to get his own way.
　　　　Determined. Resolved.
Beware if you tease him.
He's a cat. He's assuming
　　　　your job is to please him.

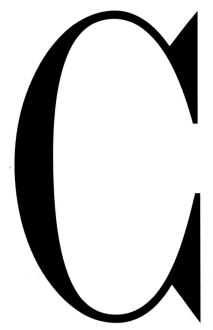

C connotes Cleo,
    who rests in the yard.
Oh, the life of a cat's
    so exhausting, so hard.

    Mice and birds to annoy;
        Bowls of milk you must lap;
All those gardens to play in
    before you can nap.

D denotes Duchess,
　　　a fine Siamese.
Her home's one of luxury,
comfort, and ease;
　　　with satins, with pillows
upon which will set
　　　the sleek, dainty paws
　　　　　of this patrician pet.

's for Eddy
             of rascally ilk.

It's not such a shock
             he's knocked over some milk.

                    Maybe he feels
       a twinge of guilt,
                         but why cry over
       what's already spilt?

F features Fred,
a scholarly fellow;
his temperament thoughtful,
contemplative, mellow.
This evening he's taking
a studious look
at one of his favorites,
a science book.

G, oh, Gina,

indolent, she,
who lounges about
taking pastries and tea.

A daily habit
of breakfast in bed
has caused Gina's once-slender figure
to spread.

H is Harry:

What might we suppose
he's dreaming about,
in tranquil repose?
How peaceful, how calm
his meditation.
A feline example
of pure relaxation.

I is for Ivan,
who wants a sardine
to vary his regular
tuna routine.

If only he had
an opposable thumb
he could pick up that key
and get himself some.

J is Jack,
packed to go.
A jaunt to Paris?
Tokyo?
Maybe Manhattan?
A voyage to Rome?

[The truth of it is he has to stay home.]

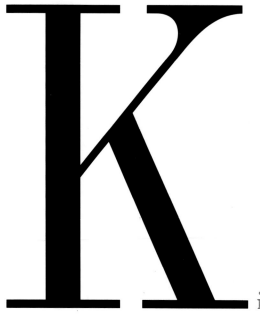K is for Kitty,

up on the shelf,
next to the mirror,
beside herself;
with sunlight streaming
through the lace,
and garden blossoms
in a vase.

L is for Lily,

a beautiful sight;

a spare composition of

white on white.

With looks like hers,

no more is required

than just to sit

and be admired.

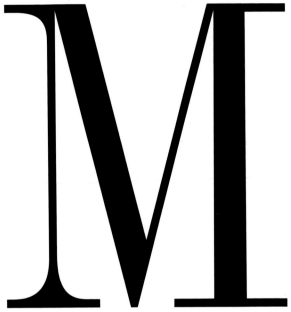 is for Maude.

Unruffled she poses
for a picture called
"Tortoiseshell Cat and Roses."

N is for Nora,
grand lady, refined.
On shrimp and salmon
this evening she's dined.
Now, in an elegant,
velvety mood,
we'll play her a waltz
and a Chopin prelude.

O is Olivia,

looking up,
standing by
her golden cup.

Not an issue
in dispute
is the fact
that she is cute.

P points to Peter
whose people ensure
his exposure to
culture and literature.
Never lacking
books to read
make his thoughts
profound, indeed.
Food for thought
has this appeal:
He thinks of more
than his next meal.

Q is for Quincie,
waiting on top
of the counter
for any spare tidbits; a chop,
or a trout,
or a gizzard to chew....
Too bad; tonight's menu's
a vegetable stew.

R stands for Raymond.
He's dapper and neat
as he sits for a spell
in his window seat.

What happier way
to spend an hour
than by curling one's tail
and smelling a flower?

 is Sinclair.

He's that rare kind of chap
who's at home anywhere,
in a crowd, on your lap.

Amidst chaos and blare,
among flowers and fruit,
his poise is assured.
His aplomb's absolute.

T is for Tess,
a country gal;
a forthright friend,
a homespun pal.
Amiability
she'll display

[unless you're a small, rural target of prey].

U
is Ulysses;
indoors he stays
on cold and wintry
London days.

Heavy petting,
a cozy fire,
are what such
afternoons require.

V is Valentina,
with an ardent glance.
She lives with an artist
in the south of France.
When he sells a painting,
for an extra centime,
they dine at a café
on kibbles and cream.

W's Willa,

a creature who's
sitting on what you'd
planned to peruse.
Each Sunday morning
she'll make you choose:
Her whims and comfort,
or your news?

X is Xavier.
He's tuckered out.
Did he, or the yarn,
get the best of this bout?

No doubt that they'll go
yet another round
and wrestle till
one or the other's unwound.

is Yves

who had a hunch
"No" would be the answer to
"Let's do lunch?"

At the moment he asked
this indelicate question,
the fish swam away
in an opposite direction.

Z is for Zeus,

a splendid version

of the breed that is known as

Golden Persian.

Honor paid this

eminent pet

brings us to the end

of the alphabet.

Special thanks to
Tony Wessling and Barbara Flynn,
and to our
editors, Kathy Belden and
Valerie Kuscenko.

And in grateful acknowledgment
to Caroline Fletcher,
Doug Flynn,
Terence Flynn,
Beth and Meghan Flynnperrault,
Carol Hacker,
Robin Haines, Greg Jesser,
Lisa Kruse,
Mary Lawrence,
Susan and Nicholas McGlibery,
Ninepatch, Marge Ponting,
Bill Porter,
Russell Pritchard at Zonal,
Evelyn Randolph,
Denis and Marsha Roberge,
Alex Sanso,
The Solano Pet Shop, Kay Spang,
Tail of the Yak,
Top Dog, and Gene Vick.

A  Z

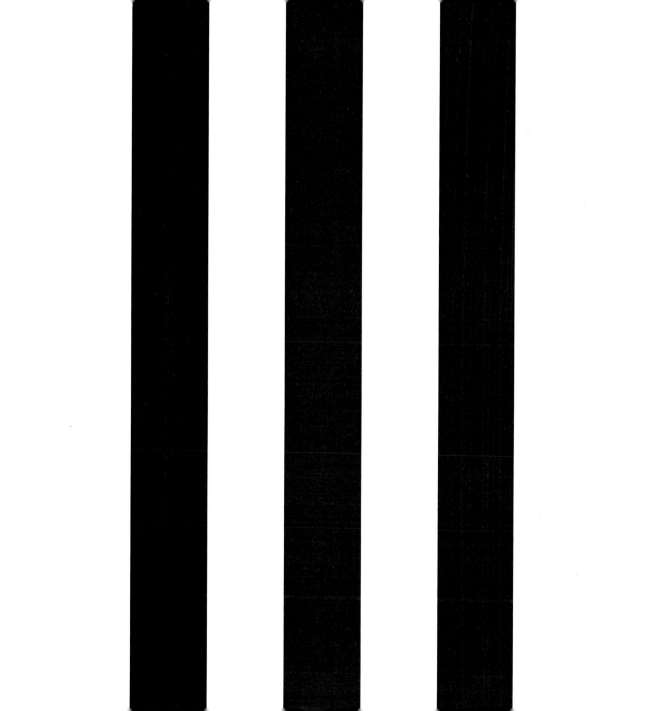

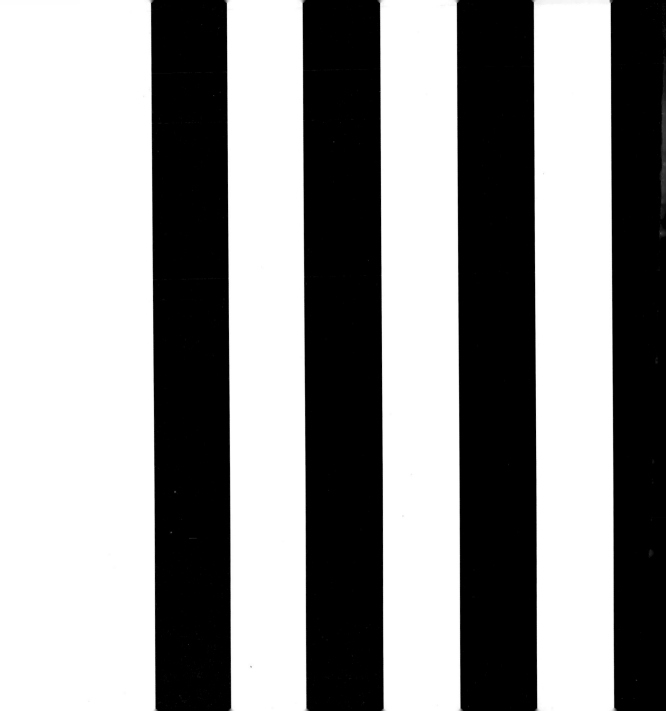